Presented to

....

From

....

On this date

....

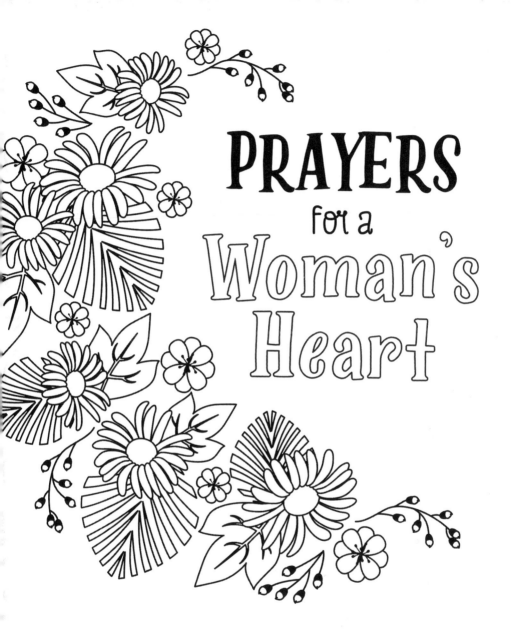

PRAYERS
for a
Woman's Heart

➤➤➤ Creative Devotional ⧐⧐⧐

BARBOUR BOOKS
An Imprint of Barbour Publishing, Inc.

Prayers written by Anna Bailee, Renae Brumbaugh, Jean Fischer, Shanna Gregor, Linda Holloway, Marcia Hornok, Missy Horsfall, MariLee Parrish, and Janet Ramsdell Rockey.

Published by Barbour Books, an imprint of Barbour Publishing, Inc., 1810 Barbour Drive, Uhrichsville, Ohio 44683, www.barbourbooks.com.

Our mission is to inspire the world with the life-changing message of the Bible.

Member of the
Evangelical Christian
Publishers Association

Printed in the United States of America.

⇾⇾⇾ Color Yourself Inspired ⇽⇽⇽

Experience the beautiful prayers of a faithful heart with the *Prayers for a Woman's Heart Creative Devotional*. Featuring 52 powerful, devotional-like prayers complemented by creative coloring pages, this beautiful volume provides calming comfort and encouragement for your soul. Still your heart and mind as you reflect on these refreshing prayers—and be drawn ever closer to the One who holds the whole world in His hands.

⤐⟫⟩ My Unbelief ⟨⟨⟨⟵

So He asked his father, "How long has this been happening to him?"
And he said, "From childhood. And often he has thrown him both into
the fire and into the water to destroy him. But if You can do anything,
have compassion on us and help us." Jesus said to him, "If you can believe,
all things are possible to him who believes." Immediately the
father of the child cried out and said with tears,
"Lord, I believe; help my unbelief!"

MARK 9:21–24 NKJV

Heavenly Father, time and time again I have seen Your hand at work. Again and again You have proven Yourself trustworthy. I do believe in You. I believe in who You are and in all Your power. I believe that nothing is impossible for You! I believe You are good and just and holy and that You are working with a master plan.

Like so many things, though, faith is much easier said than done. It's easy to say I believe, especially when life is good. But it's so desperately hard to really act in faith when all seems lost or the obstacles seem impossible.

Oh God, in the darkness, when I'm overwhelmed and doubting You, please shed Your light on my circumstances. Remind me who You are. Keep my focus on Your promises. Soothe my anxiety with Your peace. Please, Father, strengthen my faith in You, and help my unbelief.

Applying Wisdom

We have not stopped praying for you since the first day we heard about you. In fact, we always pray that God will show you everything he wants you to do and that you may have all the wisdom and understanding that his Spirit gives. Then you will live a life that honors the Lord, and you will always please him by doing good deeds. You will come to know God even better.

COLOSSIANS 1:9–10 CEV

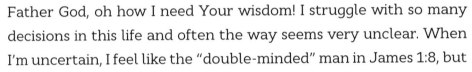

Father God, oh how I need Your wisdom! I struggle with so many decisions in this life and often the way seems very unclear. When I'm uncertain, I feel like the "double-minded" man in James 1:8, but You promise to reveal Your wisdom if I ask in faith.

As Paul prayed for believers all through the New Testament, so I pray, Lord, for wisdom and understanding of Your power and greatness. Wisdom goes beyond knowledge. Wisdom is knowledge gained by experience; it is good sense or judgment. Wisdom is experiential—it is meant to be acted upon. It goes beyond simply "knowing" something and gets to the heart of understanding it.

That's so true for my spiritual walk, Lord! I read Your Word and "know" all about You and Your ways. I may know many things—but what do I do with that knowledge? That's wisdom. Help me gain knowledge, apply wisdom, and obey Your Word so I can come to know You "even better." Amen.

⤐⟫⟫⟩ In Times of Doubt ⟨⟨⟨⟨⟤

But those who trust the Lord will find new strength. They will be strong like
eagles soaring upward on wings; they will walk and run without getting tired.
Isaiah 40:31 cev

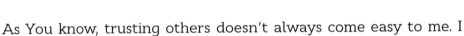

As You know, trusting others doesn't always come easy to me. I should be able to trust You, God, 100 percent, but there are difficult times that cause me to doubt. Forgive me when I struggle with that. There are people who have failed me, but You have never failed me—even when I couldn't see how things were going to turn out.

You never promised that everything would be easy. You even said in Your Word that there would be trouble, even as Your child. But You have promised that those challenges will not consume me as long as I lean and rely on You. Even in heartache or tragedy You can turn it to my good.

I choose today to trust You, no matter what the circumstances look like. You said there is nothing I can do—no circumstance in life—that will separate me from Your love. Help me to look to You and You alone. Take my hand and lead me through the difficulty. As long as I have walked with You, You have never left me without hope. You have always provided a way of escape. You always keep Your promises and so again today, I place my trust in You!

The Gift of God's Light

"The sun will no more be your light by day, nor will the brightness of the moon shine on you, for the Lord will be your everlasting light, and your God will be your glory."

ISAIAH 60:19 NIV

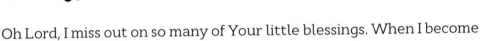

Oh Lord, I miss out on so many of Your little blessings. When I become entwined in my daily tasks, I forget to look for You. But then You open my eyes, and You shine Your loving light upon me. Every day, I see Your light all around me. I awaken to a magnificent sunrise with colors that rival the best artists' palettes. Your sunlight brightens my day and it warms me. Your light shines in children's laughter and the kind acts of strangers and friends. I see it in smiles shared and comforting words and in friendship. All through the day it shines. And when the sun sets, Lord, Your light goes on. You set the moon in the sky to softly light the earth. You scatter the stars across Your black velvet canvas. You call each star by name. I look at the night sky, and I know that You exist beyond it. I imagine Your heaven, a place where the sun always shines. And when I turn off the light before I go to sleep, I am never in darkness, because You, God, are my everlasting light. When the sun, the moon, and the stars go out, when Earth's light fails, Your light will shine forever. Amen.

⤜⤜⤜ Show Me Your Ways ⤛⤛⤛

Show me your ways, Lord, teach me your paths. Guide me in your truth and teach me, for you are God my Savior, and my hope is in you all day long.

PSALM 25:4-5 NIV

———————●————————————————●———————

Show me Your ways, Lord. Guide me and teach me the truth. Help me to put my hope in You no matter what. I think about Job and all he endured. He lost everything, and yet he still put his trust in You. He was stripped down to nothing and even his health was failing. His wife told him to curse You and die! Yet Job still held on to the hope that You were sovereign and that You were with him. You were faithful to Job and restored to him all that was lost and more. Job said, "I had only heard about You before, but now I have seen You with my own eyes." Help me to have the kind of faith that Job had.

I know my faith will be tested in many ways as I live life in this fallen world. Continue to guide me in Your truth. I know I will fail at some point, and I am so thankful that You are gracious and compassionate, slow to anger and rich in love. Your grace is sufficient for me. Your power is made perfect in weakness. I believe as the scriptures say "when I am weak, then I am strong." I know that strength comes from You alone. Thank You, Jesus!

Always Rejoicing

Rejoice evermore. Pray without ceasing. In every thing give thanks: for this is the will of God in Christ Jesus concerning you.

1 Thessalonians 5:16-18 kjv

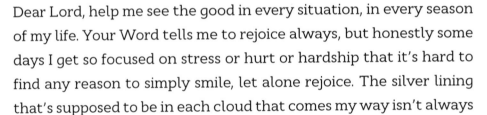

Dear Lord, help me see the good in every situation, in every season of my life. Your Word tells me to rejoice always, but honestly some days I get so focused on stress or hurt or hardship that it's hard to find any reason to simply smile, let alone rejoice. The silver lining that's supposed to be in each cloud that comes my way isn't always very shiny.

In those times when I'm struggling to find any joy, help me to stop and gain a better perspective. I know I have plenty to be thankful for. I have so much to rejoice over and praise You for. I have life and breath and promises from You to provide for every need and to never leave or forsake me. Help me to realize that You are all I need. Every other good thing in my life is simply an added bonus because I have it all in You!

Keep me in constant communication with You. And thank You that You, the God of the universe, want to be in constant communication with me. When I keep my focus on that fact, when I keep my focus on You, how can I help but rejoice always? You are amazing, God!

Compassion for Others

According as he hath chosen us in him before the foundation of the world,

that we should be holy and without blame before him in love.

EPHESIANS 1:4 KJV

Lord, sometimes I struggle to see the good in people. I can be quick to judge. Then I remember all I was before I knew the great sacrifice You made for me. I pray You will let me see others through Your eyes. All You have done for me, You have also done for them—even if they have not accepted Your gift yet.

I was dead in my sin, but You have made me alive in Christ. So when others do things that offend me, help me to forgive them because You willingly forgave me. So many times I disappointed You, but You responded in mercy. Help me to show mercy to those who disappoint me. There was a time when I followed the world instead of You. I pray that those who don't know You will find You, just as I did. Help me to stand for truth and believe that someday those who choose deceit can know Your truth as well.

I stand in faith now, praying that those deceived by Satan will find freedom in Christ. That they may know Your love and learn to serve You. Pour out Your compassion and love into my heart so that I may respond with a heart of wisdom toward those You give me opportunity to point toward You today.

Watch Jesus

We must keep our eyes on Jesus, who leads us and makes our faith complete.

HEBREWS 12:2 CEV

Dear Father, our world—okay, my world—is distracting! Rush here. Rush there. Multitask. Street construction. And then there's technology.

I'm always feeling behind. The rug needs vacuuming. The car needs washing. I ought to check email and Facebook at least three or four times a day. After all, I'm on two prayer teams. I must call friends. Set coffee dates. Where is that get-well card I bought yesterday?

I think I may talk too much when I get together with friends. I should try to listen more.

Oops! I seemed to have veered off track. Distracted again.

Urgency is a thief! Lord, I want to live life deliberately. Not haphazardly, worn out from attending to the next squeaky wheel. Help me prioritize. And please help me ignore the snarky voice that whispers, "You're going to be late. You should have left five minutes ago. Hurry!"

Maybe if I would keep my eyes on Jesus, anxiety couldn't gain a foothold. Otherwise it's all about me, working hard to please who? Whom? (See? Distracted again.)

Jesus, because of You I don't have to allow distractions to pull me off course. Your Holy Spirit will lead me. I can trust Him. What's important today? I've got my to-do list, but what's Yours?

How Wide, How Long, How High, How Deep!

And may you have the power to understand, as all God's people should, how wide, how long, how high, and how deep his love is. May you experience the love of Christ, though it is too great to understand fully. Then you will be made complete with all the fullness of life and power that comes from God.

EPHESIANS 3:18-19 NLT

Father God, I often feel like I don't deserve Your love for me. It's unconditional and relentless. It pursues me when I pretend I can do without it. It accepts me and forgives me and welcomes me back repeatedly. Sometimes I feel sure You should just give up on me, but thankfully You never do. I can't imagine where I'd be if not for Your unfailing love, and it's impossible for me to put into words how grateful I am for that.

I know I will never understand Your love fully, but please help me to keep experiencing it in new ways every single day. Surprise me with it. Sustain me with it. Comfort me with it. Satisfy me with it. Let it fill me up to overflowing—and let me share it with others! Help me to crave Your love above any other thing so that I am in constant communication and relationship with You through prayer and through Your Word. You are love itself, God. I praise You, and I love You back.

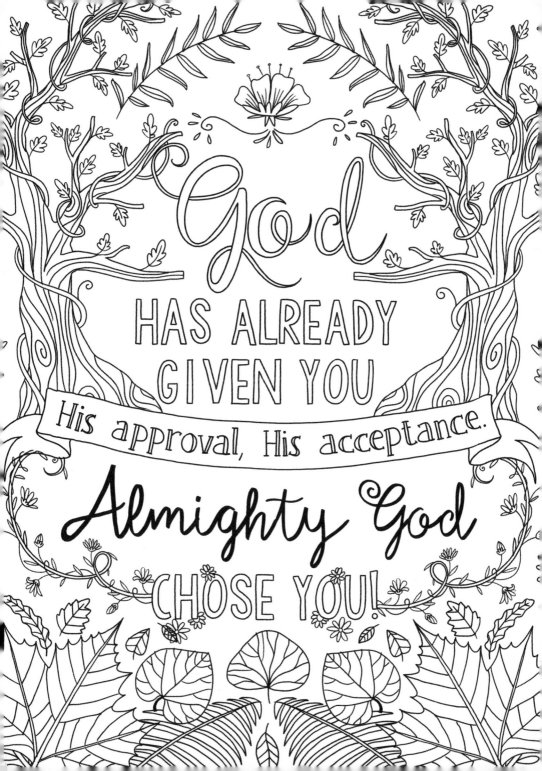

Wow Me with Your Power, God

Now all glory to God, who is able, through his mighty power at work within us, to accomplish infinitely more than we might ask or think. Glory to him in the church and in Christ Jesus through all generations forever and ever! Amen.

EPHESIANS 3:20-21 NLT

Almighty God, please remind me of Your power. I tend to put You in a box, expecting You to work in only the ways I can think up. I worry through a problem, trying to apply only the figures and formulas that make sense to me, but that's kind of ridiculous—for You are the Creator of the universe, capable of so much more than I can possibly wrap my mind around. Your Word promises me You are able to do infinitely more than all I can ask or imagine.

Please wow me as You work in my current situation, as only You can do. Exceed all my expectations. Amaze me in a new way. Show me that absolutely nothing is impossible for You. I want to see Your hand at work, and I want to give all praise and honor to You. I want others to see Your miraculous ways, to witness Your almighty power, and I want You to receive all the glory!

Heart Needs

Give me an undivided heart, that I may fear your name.

PSALM 86:11 NIV

God of my hope, it amazes me that I belong to You for all eternity, but life here is hard. Thank You for temporal pleasures, pleasant emotions, significant accomplishments, and meaningful relationships. But everything ages and atrophies. My heart must be set on pilgrimage, not on corruptible things. What I trust in place of You—people, possessions, activities, accomplishments, investments—is a counterfeit and an illusion. My joy is in You, not in what I do or who I love. I can rejoice in You, even when not feeling joyful.

God of my expectations, tame my wandering heart. I know that may necessitate a broken heart, but Your will be done. How easily distracted I am by self-seeking goals and my desire for approval from peers. I can realize the certain hope of my calling and the constant reality of Your power only when I fix my eyes on You: on Your glory, not my needs; on Your loyal love, regardless of my feelings. Help me to live devotionally, meditating on all You are and what You speak to me when I read Your Word. Although I fear trials and future sorrows, help me remember I can endure anything because You are always with me, Your Word is adequate, and Your grace is sufficient. Tears teach lessons I could not learn any other way. My whole heart loves You. Amen.

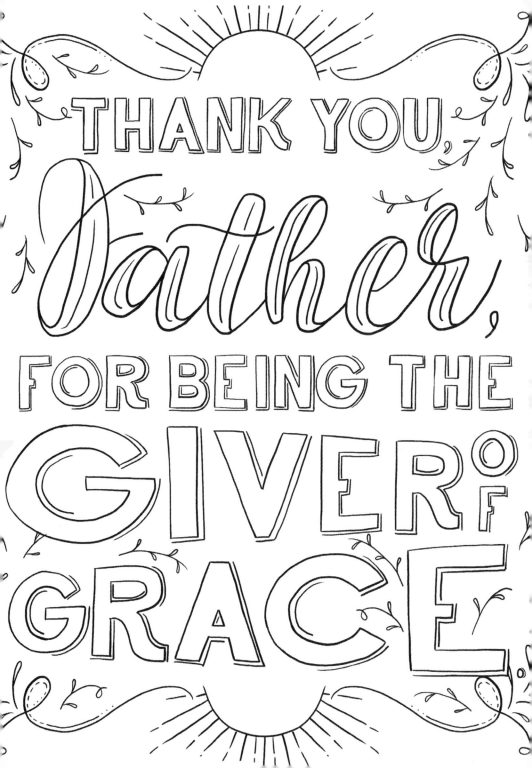

Confident Hope

Guide me in your truth and teach me, for you are
God my Savior, and my hope is in you all day long.

PSALM 25:5 NIV

God, what would I do without You? When my spirit is weak, You give me strength. When I feel hopeless, You flood my heart with Your light, and You fill me up with hope. My hope is in You, God, always and forever.

When I travel a road long and hard, You are there at my side. You encourage me and keep me moving forward with hope. When I face a task overwhelmed and worried, thinking that it is too much for me, You give me hope and confidence to succeed. And when night falls, silent and dark, You light my way with the confident hope that morning will surely come.

Who would I be, God, without You? Hope in myself is not enough. I fail, and my spirit falls desperate. But You, God—You give me hope! Even when the world says there is none, there is always hope in Christ Jesus, Your Son. What a wonderful gift He is, Your gift of hope to the world. He took all of my sins, died with them, and then rose from the dead to give me hope. My hope is in You, God; my trust is in Jesus. Thank You for the confident hope that one day I will enter the gates of heaven and live there with You forever. Amen.

Growing in Love and Knowledge

But I am like a green olive tree in the house of God. I trust in the steadfast love of God forever and ever. I will thank you forever, because you have done it. I will wait for your name, for it is good, in the presence of the godly.

PSALM 52:8–9 ESV

Heavenly Father, I will thank You forever! Anything good I have in my life is from You and for You. And the amazing thing is that You have even taken the bad and turned it into good! You turned my ashes into beauty and my shame into joy. You have promised freedom from chains. . .and peace from despair. You have faithfully fulfilled those promises in my life.

Like the olive tree, You are showing me how to grow in a healthy and right relationship with You and with others. You want me to flourish. You are for me, so who can be against me? It doesn't matter what anyone else thinks as long as I know in my heart that I'm pleasing You.

Help me to be strong in You when You ask me to do things that friends and family don't understand. Sometimes the cost of following You seems too much to bear. Please remind me that the rewards of following You are eternal. Keep me growing in the love and knowledge of You.

⊱⊱⊱ The Journey of Faith ⊰⊰⊰

Stop being hateful! Quit trying to fool people, and start being sincere. Don't be jealous or say cruel things about others. Be like newborn babies who are thirsty for the pure spiritual milk that will help you grow and be saved. You have already found out how good the Lord really is.

1 Peter 2:1-3 cev

Lord, I've been on this faith journey for a while now, and the older I get, the more I realize how much I have yet to learn. Maturity brings the realization of just how much more growth I need. Sometimes I feel like I might even be regressing, needing to relearn what I've already been taught!

I don't want to be stuck as a spiritual baby, but rather to thirst for the milk of Your Word as Peter talks about—to grow in wisdom and knowledge—to have a discerning heart so that I hold fast to all that Your Word teaches. Lord, help me gain understanding of Your character, of who You are, and to stay focused on not only learning about You, but on being transformed and changed by what I discover.

I am so thankful You are willing to help me! I know that growth can sometimes be uncomfortable and change can be painful, but I want to remember that these things are necessary and ultimately for my good. God, give me strength in heart and mind to continue on this journey of learning to know You. Amen.

Thanks for Encouragers

Therefore encourage one another and build each other up, just as in fact you are doing. Now we ask you, brothers and sisters, to acknowledge those who work hard among you, who care for you in the Lord and who admonish you. Hold them in the highest regard in love because of their work. Live in peace with each other. And we urge you, brothers and sisters, warn those who are idle and disruptive, encourage the disheartened, help the weak, be patient with everyone. Make sure that nobody pays back wrong for wrong, but always strive to do what is good for each other and for everyone else.

1 Thessalonians 5:11-15 niv

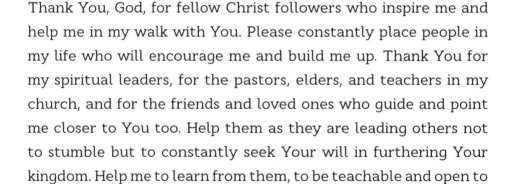

Thank You, God, for fellow Christ followers who inspire me and help me in my walk with You. Please constantly place people in my life who will encourage me and build me up. Thank You for my spiritual leaders, for the pastors, elders, and teachers in my church, and for the friends and loved ones who guide and point me closer to You too. Help them as they are leading others not to stumble but to constantly seek Your will in furthering Your kingdom. Help me to learn from them, to be teachable and open to their instruction. And help me to be as much of an encouragement to them as they are to me.

As I learn and grow, help me to be a good leader for others, as well. I want to live my life in such a way that You are pleased and so that others who know me want to love and follow You too.

Eyes on the Blessings

All praise to God, the Father of our Lord Jesus Christ,
who has blessed us with every spiritual blessing in the
heavenly realms because we are united with Christ.

EPHESIANS 1:3 NLT

Thank You, God! I praise You and give You much thanks for the blessings You have given to me. I know I sometimes take things for granted, vent my frustration, and let disappointment overwhelm me. I want to see life through the blessings You have given me.

I could spend too much time telling You all the things I wish were better, different, or less than what I had hoped. I can sit in the dark and pout, but I know it is not Your way. I should come out into the light and give thanks. Each day I determine my attitude about my life and how I will respond. The choice is mine. I want to celebrate all the things that have brought joy and peace into my life.

Today I count my blessings. I have breath and life today. I have people who love me—and that includes You as well. I look back over my life and realize that You were always there, even the times I didn't feel Your presence. You have taken me on a journey, and You have made serious adjustments as a result of my own personal choices. No matter where I go or what I do, You are always there to show me the right path and bring Your blessings into my life.

I need your
healing and
peace,
Lord.

Sharing the Light

When Jesus spoke again to the people, he said, "I am the light of the world. Whoever follows me will never walk in darkness, but will have the light of life."

JOHN 8:12 NIV

Dear Lord, You are like a beacon of light that leads ships at sea. You light the way for the lost in the world. You give life to all who ask. Oh, how wonderful You are! You care about Your children, and You save them from death. Whenever they stray, like a good shepherd, You find them. You are their light in the darkness. "Come, follow me," You say, and then safely You lead them toward home.

I praise You, Lord Jesus. I praise You because You are the Light of the world and the light of my life. You keep my lamp burning. Every day, You flood my heart with Your love light, more than it can hold. I am eager to share it, so allow me, please, to help You to light up the world.

You are the only One who turns darkness into light. How can I share the light? How can I help the lost? What can I do to show them Your love? Lead me to them. Guide me to say and do what is right. Make me an example of Your light, and give me wisdom. Speak to me through Your Word, and help me to lead others out of their darkness so that they might live in Your light forever. Amen.

I HAVE TOLD THE GOOD NEWS ABOUT WHAT IS RIGHT and GOOD... you know I will not CLOSE MY LIPS, O LORD.

PSALM 40:9

Shining God's Light of Love

My prayer is that light will flood your hearts and that you will understand the hope that was given to you when God chose you. Then you will discover the glorious blessings that will be yours together with all of God's people.

EPHESIANS 1:18 CEV

My Father in heaven, please help me to turn away from the dark shadows of this world. They are mysterious and enticing, but You are the glorious light whose radiance casts out the darkness.

I cherish the promise of hope, which You have given to all of us whom You have chosen. I stand ready in the charge of Your calling to let Your light shine through me. You have set me apart as a member of Your heavenly family. To be called Your child is so great an honor.

As my heart is flooded with the light of Your love, let me grasp the power of Your glory. Let me eagerly pore over and study Your good Word. And let my mind and heart be open to receiving Your inheritance, an immeasurable gift of legacy. Give me the strength I'll need to pass these timeless treasures on with joy to the generations coming behind me. They so desperately need Your light.

Thank You, Lord, for showering me with the light of understanding, that I shall be able to uphold my faith in You. In Jesus' blessed name, amen.

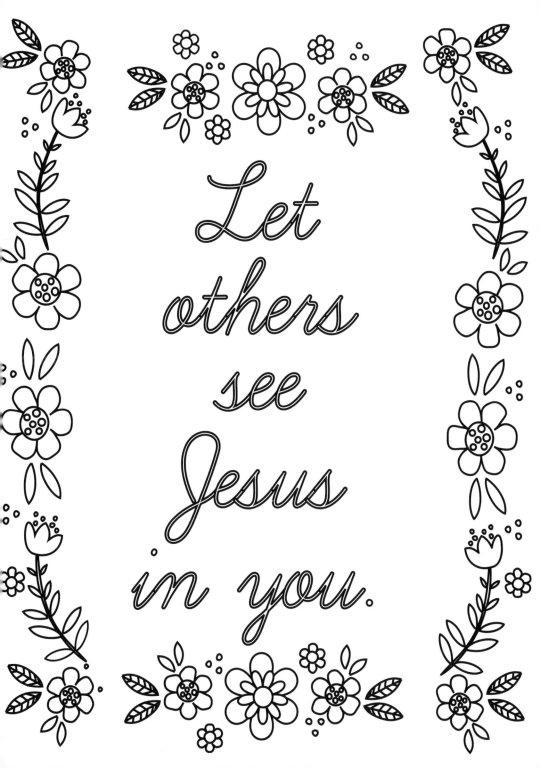

⤜⤜⤜ Praising the Power of God ⤛⤛⤛

In that day you will say: "Give praise to the Lord, proclaim his name;
make known among the nations what he has done, and proclaim that his name
is exalted. Sing to the Lord, for he has done glorious things; let this be
known to all the world. Shout aloud and sing for joy, people of Zion,
for great is the Holy One of Israel among you."

ISAIAH 12:4-6 NIV

Oh God, how mighty and powerful You are! I look around me in wonder at the mountains and oceans, the fields, deserts, canyons, and plains. You made them all just by speaking them into existence. I gaze up into an infinite breadth of blue. Clouds drift by, slow, undisturbed, and I know that the sky is Yours. You set the sun, the moon, and the stars in place. You know them all by name. When the heavens turn gray and seas go rough, then I feel Your presence. Rain falls. Lightning strikes, and yet, You protect me. Oh, how strong and loving You are! I see You in birth and also in death. No one but You, God, has the power to give life and to know exactly when it will end. I celebrate each new season and mourn its passing all the while praising You, leaning on You, and loving You. I shout Your name, and I sing Your praises. You alone are my God, the One who always was, always is, and will be forever. Amen.

God's Constant Presence

Where can I go from your Spirit? Where can I flee from your presence? If I go up to the heavens, you are there; if I make my bed in the depths, you are there. If I rise on the wings of the dawn, if I settle on the far side of the sea, even there your hand will guide me, your right hand will hold me fast.

Psalm 139:7–10 niv

Lord Jesus, sometimes I feel so alone. I start to wonder if there is anyone who understands me, and I just feel lost and unhappy with who I am. Would You change those thoughts in me and give me a new way to think? Give me the desire to get into Your Word so that You can replace those negative thoughts with Your truth.

I love these verses in the Psalms that promise me that no matter where I go, You see me and You are with me. What a huge comfort to my soul! Please change my feelings to match Your truth. I trust that Your Word is true and that no matter how I feel, the reality is that You are guiding me and Your hand is holding mine.

You are a kind and gracious God who sees me as a precious child—holy and dearly loved. Remind me of Your constant presence in my life. I am so thankful that You know and understand my wandering heart. Bring me back to the full understanding that You will never leave or forsake me.

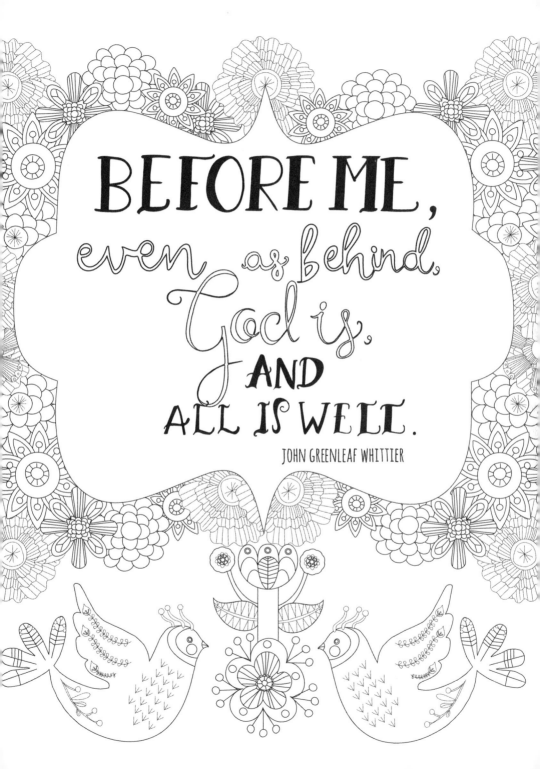

BEFORE ME, even as behind, God is, AND ALL IS WELL.

JOHN GREENLEAF WHITTIER

What Wisdom Requires

I keep asking that the God of our Lord Jesus Christ, the glorious
Father, may give you the Spirit of wisdom and revelation.

EPHESIANS 1:17 NIV

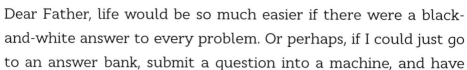

Dear Father, life would be so much easier if there were a black-and-white answer to every problem. Or perhaps, if I could just go to an answer bank, submit a question into a machine, and have Your answer for my specific situation printed out for me. . .that would be great. But life's not that simple.

Oh, You gave me guidelines. And there are some black-and-white answers in Your Book. But for most of my questions, I need to figure things out for myself. Except, I don't have to do it all by myself. You promised Your wisdom to any who asked.

Lord, wisdom requires me to seek You. Wisdom requires me to ponder and pray and act in faith, even if I'm not sure of the right answer. Wisdom requires me to take time and really think things through, rather than just reacting.

Lord, I want to have Your wisdom. I want You to reveal Your thoughts to me. I want to do things Your way instead of my own way. I know Your way is much better, by far.

Father, show me Your wisdom today. Reveal Yourself to me. Amen.

A Heart Built with Wisdom

Through wisdom is an house builded; and by understanding it is established: and by knowledge shall the chambers be filled with all precious and pleasant riches.

PROVERBS 24:3-4 KJV

God, I could spend every day building my life and my home, but if You're not included, then that life and home will not remain. Wisdom is the principal thing that I need to build my life upon. You have promised wisdom if I ask for it, and today I am asking. I need wisdom to build my life, my home, and my family.

Today I open my heart and my home to You. Come in and live with us. I want You to build the house that will not fail. As we come together each day, may Your presence be evidence among us. May Your love explode in our hearts for one another and for You.

The material things the world wants and needs fade in comparison to the rich blessings You have for us when You are the center of our world. We want to make decisions that reflect Your purpose and plan for our lives.

Let the wisdom You give us spill over from our lives and our home into the lives of others. Knit our hearts together with our extended families, friends, and even new acquaintances You bring through our doors. Let wisdom speak in every area of our lives today.

In Spite of Myself

Follow God's example, therefore, as dearly loved children and
walk in the way of love, just as Christ loved us and gave himself
up for us as a fragrant offering and sacrifice to God.

EPHESIANS 5:1-2 NIV

Lord, this walking "in the way of love" means recognizing that others are different from myself. It means offering grace—Your grace—to everyone around me. Offering grace means knowing that everyone has a story and circumstances that are unique to them. If I take the time to listen to their stories, I may find an understanding beyond my own to offer them more than what I could before.

You love me—despite myself—and because of Your unfathomable love I can offer that to others. I have begun to see that You have much to teach me through others, Lord. Help me listen and to learn. It is not my job to fix others, but to pray, and to be shaped and molded into Your image.

A "sacrifice" means a difficult choice. It is offering something that costs me. Your Son sacrificed His life for mine. Can I do less? God, help me to walk this path of love and service, of offering grace when that is a difficult choice. Your Word teaches a way that is not easy, but You promise to be all that we need to be in us. Lord, give me strength and power each day to walk in Your love. Amen.

GOD is writing A STORY of FAITH through your LIFE.

Trusting in God's Power When He Is Silent

God has spoken plainly, and I have heard
it many times: power, O God, belongs to you.

PSALM 62:11 NLT

Dear God, forgive me when I forget to trust in You. I know that You are all-powerful and all-knowing and that You love me. But sometimes my mind wanders away from You as I dwell on my problems and the things that I want. That is when I need You the most. You know my trials. You know exactly what I need. Yet when I pray You are silent, and I wonder if You hear me. I know that You are there, God! Your power is beyond my understanding. While I worry and wait, You are there working out the perfect plan to end my trials and give me exactly what I need. Why then is it hard for me to always trust in You? Why do I run on ahead of You trying to do things on my own? You are the Rock on which I stand. You are my solid ground. So help me to stand still and turn my thoughts toward You. I do not have to hear from You, again and again, to know that You have my life in Your hands. You have told me many times before. You have everything under control, and You love me. All that You do is perfect. So when You are silent, God, help me to be patient. Help me to trust in Your power and love. Amen.

A Light That Shines with Honor

Honor Christ and let him be the Lord of your life. Always be ready to give an answer when someone asks you about your hope.

1 Peter 3:15 CEV

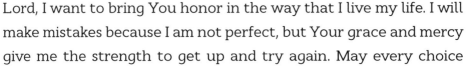

Lord, I want to bring You honor in the way that I live my life. I will make mistakes because I am not perfect, but Your grace and mercy give me the strength to get up and try again. May every choice and every decision reflect Your goodness. Help me to be of good reputation and high integrity in all that I do each day.

Like a flashlight that shows you the way to go when you find yourself walking in the forest after dark, I pray that my life will be a light that guides others in the path You have for them. Let me demonstrate Your goodness and Your mercy. I desire to be a picture of Your faithfulness.

It is my heart's desire that others will see my life as something unique and different. May they look into my heart and see the love of God that has been shed abroad in it by Your holy hand. Help me to not be moved by my emotions but by the Holy Spirit. When people look at me, I want them to see You. Let my words be loving and gentle, and my actions reflect a sincere heart to serve You in all I do.

Place
your hope
in God's goodness.

Loving God's Word

Thy word is a lamp unto my feet, and a light unto my path.

PSALM 119:105 KJV

I need Your Word every day, Lord. I need it desperately as the lamp and light to guide me in this dark world. Too often, I push time in Your Word to the side, letting all my other plans for the day take precedence, and then I wonder why I feel like I'm stumbling in the dark. You, sovereign God, should be my first priority. Help me to crave time with You first thing in the morning so I can start my day out right with eyes fixed on You, with hands and feet and head and heart ready to do Your will.

There are so many things in this life battling for my attention—most of them very demanding. But You won't force me, will You, Lord? You want my willing, devoted attention. Forgive me when my sin gets in the way of my relationship and communication with You. Thank You that You never give up, quietly nudging at my heart to draw me back to You when I stray. I want to be accountable to You and Your Word. Where I need them, please bring fellow believers into my life to help keep me accountable, and for where You have already placed them I am so grateful!

Please help my life be a testimony every single day that Your Word is living and active in me, and it is guiding every step of my way.

Inheritance

I pray that the eyes of your heart may be enlightened in order that you may know the hope to which he has called you, the riches of his glorious inheritance in his holy people.

EPHESIANS 1:18 NIV

Dear Father, sometimes I forget the true meaning of the word *hope*. I find myself hoping it doesn't rain, or hoping my team wins, or hoping I get a Christmas bonus from my boss. But hope isn't some feeble wish. The hope that comes from You is a certainty of Your goodness, an assurance of greater things to come. It's a firm, unbending belief that my future is glorious.

As Your child, I've already been written into the will. I've already been given the peace and joy and abundant life promised to Your heirs. But there's more. . .so much more to come, isn't there?

One day, I'll live with You in Your house. In that place, gold is so abundant it's poured out like concrete to build roads. In Your house, there's a mansion waiting for me. It's not a pretend, fairy-tale dream. Heaven is a real place, and You have a real inheritance for Your children.

Until then, Lord, I want to take full advantage of the inheritance I've already received. No matter what my situation, I can have peace, because peace is already mine. I can have joy, because You've already granted me full access to Your joy. Remind me of that, Lord. Amen.

More Grace for Others

Just as our bodies have many parts and each part has a
special function, so it is with Christ's body. We are many
parts of one body, and we all belong to each other.

ROMANS 12:4-5 NLT

Thank You, God, for the body of Christ. Sometimes I am disheartened by the things I hear my brothers and sisters in Christ do and say. It is difficult sometimes to walk in love and peace with them. But You desire for us to be one body. Please give me Your grace to navigate the road You have set before us. Help me to walk with them and not stand against them.

Give me the strength to be honest and direct in expressing my feelings and desires. I desire Your wisdom to say what should or should not be said that would bring about Your plan for our lives. We have one God, one faith, and are moving in the same direction.

I desire to be a blessing to everyone I meet—especially those who share my faith. Fill me with the knowledge of Your will, and give me spiritual understanding in how to love those You bring across my path. Fill me with words of encouragement and hope that inspires others to live according to Your Word. Bring us into unity and give us Your love for one another.

The Lord
will open for
you His
Good store-house,
the heavens.

—Deuteronomy 28:12

Open My Eyes

I pray that the eyes of your heart may be enlightened in order that you may know the hope to which he has called you, the riches of his glorious inheritance in his holy people.

EPHESIANS 1:18 NIV

Open my eyes, Lord. Help me to see clearly all that You have for me. It's easy to get distracted by the things around me, things that have little to do with who I am in You.

I look around and see stress, but You've given me peace. I see despair, but You've given me hope. I see myself as powerless to fight against the evil around me, but You've made me powerful.

Father, this world has created a thick film over my eyes. That film keeps Your light from shining through. It keeps me lost, and causes me to bump into things. I'm spiritually blind.

I want to see You. I want to see clearly, the way You see things, but I can't. Not without Your help. Not without Your intervention.

Perform surgery on the eyes of my heart, Lord. Remove the spiritual cataracts that cloud my vision and darken my life. I want a clear view, so Your light, Your love, Your beauty can shine through.

Give me twenty-twenty vision for the spiritual. I want to see every detail of the good things You have for me. Open my eyes, Lord. Amen.

Spiritual Wisdom through God's Word

Your teachings are wonderful, and I respect them all.
Understanding your word brings light to the minds of ordinary
people. I honestly want to know everything you teach.

PSALM 119:129-131 CEV

Heavenly Father, whenever I enter my time of Bible study, I thank You for speaking to me through Your Word. Lead me through Your scriptures and enlighten me. Help me to learn Your principles so that I may live in a way that is pleasing to You. Allow Your Word to light my path. The Bible is my map to heaven. When I am weak, it makes me strong. When I am sad, it comforts me. Your Word gives hope to the hopeless and power to the powerless. Its promises fill up my heart with joy. Oh Lord, make me wise in Your truth! Store Your words in my heart, and allow them to fill my mouth with Your praises. Make clear to me the scriptures' hidden meanings. Open my eyes to what I do not understand, for I am Your student, honestly wanting to know everything You teach. Be patient with me as I study. Repeat to me often what I need to know, and give me a firm understanding so that I can share Your wisdom with others. Please quiet my thoughts while we are together in the Word. Inspire me. Take me deeper into understanding more about You and the love that You have for me. In Jesus' name I pray. Amen.

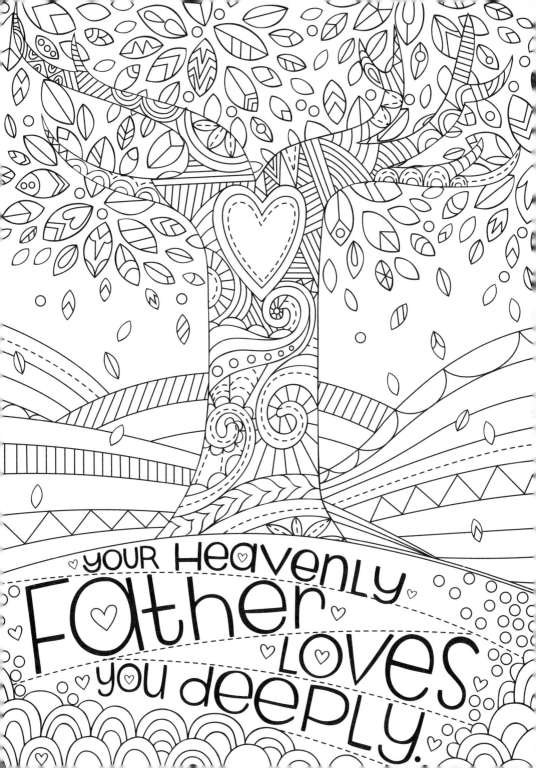

Modeling God's Love

What if I could speak all languages of humans and of angels? If I did not love others, I would be nothing more than a noisy gong or a clanging cymbal. What if I could prophesy and understand all secrets and all knowledge? And what if I had faith that moved mountains? I would be nothing, unless I loved others. What if I gave away all that I owned and let myself be burned alive? I would gain nothing, unless I loved others. Love is kind and patient, never jealous, boastful, proud, or rude. Love isn't selfish or quick tempered. It doesn't keep a record of wrongs that others do. Love rejoices in the truth, but not in evil. Love is always supportive, loyal, hopeful, and trusting. Love never fails!

1 Corinthians 13:1–8 cev

Heavenly Father, please give me Your love for people. Help me to see them as You do. I get frustrated and impatient with others too quickly. I get tired of helping them with seemingly the same problems over and over. But You love unconditionally. You love tirelessly. You love in all the ways described in this passage of scripture. Thank You for Your amazing love! I desperately need Your help to model it.

If I don't love, then anything I say I'm doing for You is meaningless. Please work in my heart and teach me what Your real love is and let me share it with others consistently.

The Same Power

That you may know the hope to which he has called you,
the riches of his glorious inheritance in his holy people,
and his incomparably great power for us who believe.

EPHESIANS 1:18–19 NIV

———

Dear Father, sometimes I forget how much power You've given me. Oh sure. I know I can overcome the little things. But I often think of my faith in You like a little energy shot. . .a tiny boost of caffeine when I'm exhausted. But that doesn't even scratch the surface, does it?

Your power took a dead man and brought Him back to life. Your power took that same man and seated Him at Your right hand. Your power commands the winds, keeps the oceans in check, holds back hell's fury.

Why do I walk around worrying about the future, fretting about this or that, intimidated by little problems that roll into my path? You can make those problems disappear. Or You will make me strong enough to get through them.

Thank You for Your power, Lord. Remind me today and every day that though I can't move mountains, I have access to the One who can. You live closer than my own heartbeat, and You lean forward to hear my every whisper. I don't have to rely on my own power. . .I simply need to trust You. Amen.

Lord, draw me always closer to You.

⇛⇛ Undeserved Gifts ⇚⇚

What do you have that you did not receive? Now if you did indeed receive it, why do you boast as if you had not received it?

1 Corinthians 4:7 NKJV

God of my blessings, thank You for the Holy Spirit indwelling me, illuminating scripture, and revealing You in its pages. You have enlightened the eyes of my heart to enable me to love You deeply and follow You closely. I take no credit for wisdom, knowledge, insight, lessons learned, or maturity gained. Everything I have is an undeserved gift from You. Spiritual fruit is a result of Your mysterious work in my life, not a reward I have earned or something I can produce. The truth that You desire me to know You, that You allow me to scratch the surface in understanding a quarter molecule of Your attributes—such knowledge is too wonderful. It is high. I cannot attain to it. Nor can I repay You, but please accept my gratitude as a sacrifice of praise.

Thank You for all the ways You show up each day. You oversee my circumstances, create opportunities, prevent calamities, and empower me to choose what is best. You also suffer with me and understand my emotions. You waste nothing. Every hard thing in life draws me closer to You and conforms me to Christ. Bless the Lord, oh my soul. Make me a light to show others Your goodness and excellence. You alone are worthy of our praise. Amen.

Don't Get Down

Why are you cast down, O my soul? And why are you disquieted within me?
Hope in God; for I shall yet praise Him, the help of my countenance and my God.

PSALM 43:5 NKJV

Dear God, I don't want to get stuck in pity parties for myself. It's so easy to complain and make a big deal about even the smallest obstacles and frustrations. Not to mention all the big ones! Please help me break that terrible habit and get out of the funks I tend to put myself in. I like things to go according to my plans. I like to set goals and work for them without any hindrance. Yet it's no secret that life rarely goes exactly according to plan—and getting depressed about it sure won't help matters. Help me to choose a good attitude and put my hope in You no matter what comes my way. It's not easy, but if You help me keep my eyes on You and praise You, I can do it!

I love what the apostle Paul said in his letter to the Romans: "May the God of hope fill you with all joy and peace as you trust in him, so that you may overflow with hope by the power of the Holy Spirit" (Romans 15:13 NIV). You are the God of hope, and when life has me discouraged and anxious, I need You to fill me with Your joy and peace. I trust in You, God! Thank You for being my one true hope!

My Gracious God

So then, since we have a great High Priest who has entered heaven,
Jesus the Son of God, let us hold firmly to what we believe. This High
Priest of ours understands our weaknesses, for he faced all of the same
testings we do, yet he did not sin. So let us come boldly to the
throne of our gracious God. There we will receive his mercy,
and we will find grace to help us when we need it most.

HEBREWS 4:14-16 NLT

Lord, sometimes I feel I need to pray like Ezra of the Old Testament: "I am too ashamed and disgraced, my God, to lift up my face to you, because our sins are higher than our heads and our guilt has reached to the heavens" (Ezra 9:6 NIV). I have messed up so many times. The guilt in my heart eats away at me and prevents me from living in freedom and joy. Help me to trust the fact that You convict my heart, but You don't condemn me. You sent Jesus to take away all my guilt and shame so that I can live in joyful freedom while You guide my steps.

You are a gracious God that looks on me with love. You see me through the cross of Christ and I no longer need to feel ashamed in Your presence. Jesus paid the price for my past, present, and future sins, and now I can boldly come into Your presence in a right relationship with You.

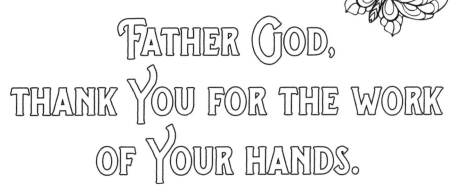

Father God, thank You for the work of Your hands.

Now and Forever

Far above all principality and power and might and dominion, and every name that is named, not only in this age but also in that which is to come.

EPHESIANS 1:21 NKJV

Eternal Father, You appeared to the world in ancient times in the form of the perfect man of Jesus. You bless us in the present age by appearing through Your holy scriptures.

You have given us a history filled with promises of hope for our future. Yet we tend to focus on the present. We often neglect our reading of the testimonies described in the Bible of man's constant battle with sin and Your abiding forgiveness. We sometimes dismiss our eternal future, selfishly contemplating our next few earthly moments. Help us to remember that our existence on earth is only for a moment. Our hope is in eternity.

Let us not be like the tares that are gathered up and burned at the end of this age, but to use what talents You have generously bestowed upon us during this life to further the spread of the Gospel of our Savior.

We give thanks for the abundant resources of Your blessings to us in Christ Jesus. Let us live in a manner today that honors You so that we may provide a true representation of Your grace for those who follow us in the future.

I pray this in the name of Jesus Christ, who was and is and is to come—the Alpha and the Omega. Amen.

Your Bounty

Every good gift and every perfect gift is from above,
and comes down from the Father of lights.

JAMES 1:17 NKJV

Bless the Lord, oh my soul. All that is within me blesses Your holy name. You have been bountiful to me. You forgive and redeem me. You crown me with Your loyal love and kindness so that I am satisfied in You. I recall all Your benefits, and it renews and refreshes me. Praise the Lord, oh my soul. You are the God of my daily benefits. Help me not to doubt You or to think You are not enough.

Forgive me for believing I'm entitled to Your blessings. And for feeling slighted when You withhold what I have begged You for, while others seem to get it without striving. I'm sorry for coveting and comparing and complaining. I deserve nothing from You. Everything I have is a bonus—every breath, every hair, every relationship, every ability and accomplishment—it all belongs to You. You are the Source of all my gifts, and You deserve all my appreciation. Yours is the glory. Train my focus away from what I don't have, what I used to have, what I could have, to make me thankful for what I do have because of Your generous grace. May I never cease giving thanks or being grateful for the hope of Your calling, the riches of Your glory, and the greatness of Your power. Bless the Lord, oh my soul. Amen.

To Reflect Him More

"If you had known Me, you would have known My Father also; and from now on you know Him and have seen Him."

JOHN 14:7 NKJV

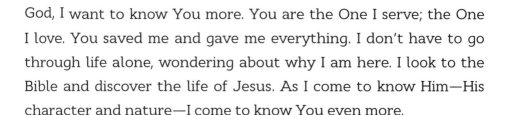

God, I want to know You more. You are the One I serve; the One I love. You saved me and gave me everything. I don't have to go through life alone, wondering about why I am here. I look to the Bible and discover the life of Jesus. As I come to know Him—His character and nature—I come to know You even more.

As I study the lives of the men and women in the Bible and the choices they made, I realize I can trust You to keep Your promises. I want to be a doer of Your Word. Help me to keep Your principles first place in my heart. May my actions and decisions reflect who You are.

Thank You for time in prayer where You speak to my heart and give me instruction and peace. I pray to be more Spirit led as I learn to follow Your voice. Thank You for Your Holy Spirit that speaks to my spirit and leads me. I am determined to listen and act on the things that You lead me to do and say.

Thank You for Your peace that brings understanding to my heart and allows me to walk by faith each day. I want to know You more. Help me to grow each day closer to You!

Child of the King

*He raised Christ from the dead and seated him at his right
hand in the heavenly realms, far above all rule and authority,
power and dominion, and every name that is invoked,
not only in the present age but also in the one to come.*

EPHESIANS 1:20-21 NIV

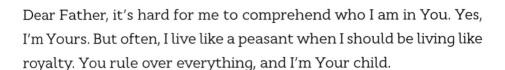

Dear Father, it's hard for me to comprehend who I am in You. Yes, I'm Yours. But often, I live like a peasant when I should be living like royalty. You rule over everything, and I'm Your child.

Lord, Your Son has been placed above every authority, every power, every dominion. . .and I'm a joint heir with Christ. I'm Your adopted child, which makes me part of the royal family.

Just as an earthly prince or princess wouldn't beg in the streets or be bullied by lowlifes, I don't have to be bullied by ungodly people or circumstances. I can go to You, my Father, and Christ, my brother, and take control of any situation. My standing holds prestige. My placement in Your family comes with privilege.

When Satan tries to intimidate me, remind me who I am. When I feel oppressed by circumstances, call to mind Your strength. Send Your Holy Spirit to advise me how to use my placement in Your family. I know You don't want me living like a peasant anymore. You want me to live like a child of the King. Amen.

Praising God's Love

For I am convinced that neither death nor life, neither angels
nor demons, neither the present nor the future, nor any powers,
neither height nor depth, nor anything else in all creation,
will be able to separate us from the love of God
that is in Christ Jesus our Lord.

ROMANS 8:38-39 NIV

Oh God, how great Your love is! Your love for me is so powerful that nothing can stop or weaken it. It reaches beyond all circumstances. Nothing on earth, past, present, or future, can take it away. You created me out of love. Your love formed me in my mother's womb. It gave me life! You love me unconditionally. When I disobey You, whenever I sin, You forgive and correct me with love. Your love desires nothing but goodness for me, and Your love leads me through the valleys. You love me so much that You sent Jesus to save me from death. He gave His life, all that He could give, because You knew that I would continue to disappoint You by sinning. Out of love, You sent Jesus so that I could be forgiven and live forever with You in heaven. Oh Father, how great Your love is! It warms my heart and brightens my days. It motivates me to love others the way that You love me—faithfully, forgivingly, and unconditionally. I praise You, God, because You are good. Your love endures forever. Thank You, God, for Your infinite love! Amen.

Praise the Lord, O my SOUL.

Psalm 103:2

Being Still

Be still, and know that I am God; I will be exalted
among the nations, I will be exalted in the earth!

PSALM 46:10 NKJV

Oh Lord, You are my refuge and strength, my fortress and strong tower, my defender and deliverer. Please fight my battles today while I stop struggling and wait on You. Take my fears and troubles. May I not be overcome by the conflicts around me, the pressures on me, and the wars within me. Give me peace in the midst of whatever chaos I encounter today, and help me to handle it all by depending on You for wisdom and understanding.

God of grace and glory, I grieve over this country's conflicts and over wars throughout the world. Starving people, persecuted Christians, children being hurt and victimized. Meet the needs of the oppressed. Give them grace and endurance, help and hope. Show me how to do my part to encourage the grieving and strengthen the weak. Break the bow and spear and be exalted by all nations, as You promised. Your Word says to be still—to cease striving—and know that You are the one true God who fights for us. Your power exceeds all greatness. You are almighty over everything, even Satan. Help me remember he is a defeated enemy who has no power over me. I exalt You. Be exalted in the world. May Your will be done on earth as it is in heaven. Amen.

Unity of Heart

That we henceforth be no more children, tossed to and fro, and carried about
with every wind of doctrine, by the sleight of men, and cunning craftiness,
whereby they lie in wait to deceive; but speaking the truth in love,
may grow up into him in all things, which is the head, even Christ.

Ephesians 4:14-15 KJV

Lord, I am a part of Your body and I represent You in all that I say and do. I know from the Bible that it is Your desire for believers to work together and bless one another. The words I speak and that others speak to me are important to both my relationship with You and with them.

When others speak to me, let me hear what You would have me hear. Let me be slow to anger and full of mercy and grace. And if the words of others hurt or condemn, then help me to let go of those words quickly and forgive the one who said them. Show me how to guard my heart from those things I don't need to hear.

I pray my words are truth and life to all who hear them. Help me by Your Holy Spirit to speak words that bring good things into people's lives. When I need to say something that will be difficult for others to hear, please give me the right words that will speak directly into the heart of the hearer and bring about Your purpose and desire for his or her life.

⤜⤜⤜ No Need for Pity ⤛⤛⤛

If Christ has not been raised, then your faith is useless and
you are still guilty of your sins. In that case, all who have died
believing in Christ are lost! And if our hope in Christ is only for
this life, we are more to be pitied than anyone in the world.
But in fact, Christ has been raised from the dead.

1 Corinthians 15:17-20 nlt

Jesus, thank You for Your resurrection! I praise You that You are worthy of my faith in You because You did, in fact, raise to life. You overcame death, and because of that, You offer us hope for eternal life too. There are many religions with many prophets and leaders with claims to providing the way to God and heaven, but You are the one true Source of real hope. Believing in You is the one true religion. You are the Way, the Truth, and the Life, and no one comes to the Father except through You. Thank You that You have already done the work that is required to be a follower of You. There are no works to be done to receive Your salvation; it's simply a matter of accepting the gift You offer by grace.

Thank You, that as a follower of You, I am not to be pitied more than all others. Help me to share the real and only hope of Your resurrection in unapologetic but always loving ways.

When I Don't Understand

May the God of hope fill you with all joy and peace
as you trust in him, so that you may overflow
with hope by the power of the Holy Spirit.

ROMANS 15:13 NIV

Lord, so much is beyond my understanding. Why do bad things happen to good people? Why do the evil prosper? Why do some suffer from illnesses while others are cured? You are a good and loving God. I believe that with all my heart. When I pray, I know that You hear me. Yet sometimes I feel disappointed when You don't answer my prayers in the way that I want. I don't understand why You allow evil to roam the earth. But Lord, there is one thing that I do know—You understand. You know the answers to all my questions. Your answers are hidden from me now, but one day I will know. You will enlighten me with Your wisdom and truth. My hope and trust are in You. When I see evil reign and I ask why, I know that You will send Your Holy Spirit to soothe me and bring me joy and peace. When Your answers are too wise for my understanding, I know that the power of Your Holy Spirit will give me hope. Oh God, how grateful I am that You are in control. I know that in the end all evil will cease and everything on earth and in heaven will exist in harmony with You. Amen.

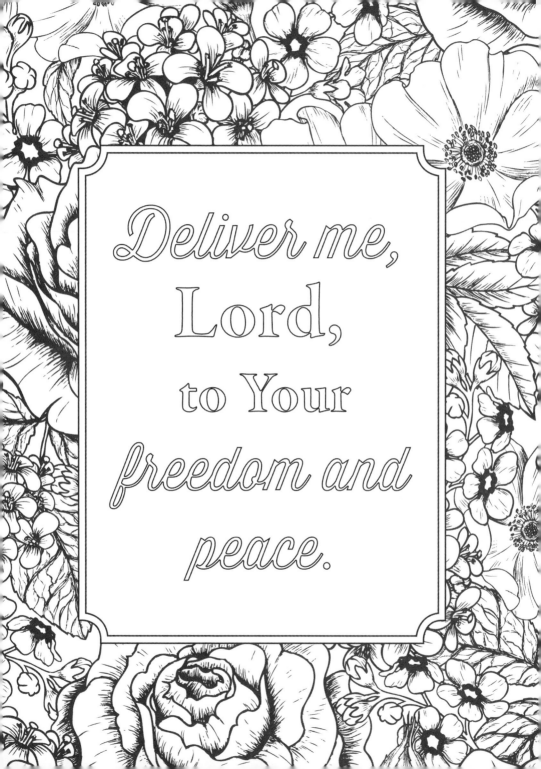

Any Circumstance

He heals the brokenhearted and bandages their wounds. He counts
the stars and calls them all by name. How great is our Lord!
His power is absolute! His understanding is beyond comprehension!

PSALM 147:3–5 NLT

Lord, I confess that I am full of questions longing to be answered. There is so much I don't understand. I battle doubts and fear; I see suffering and evil and ask, "Why?" I listen for Your voice and hear only silence. But You are neither hard of hearing nor lacking in compassion! The psalmist tells us that Your arm can save, that Your power is absolute, and that we cannot fully comprehend You.

Father, I am thankful that You are beyond the ability of my finite mind to understand and comprehend. Your majesty, might, holiness, righteousness, grace, mercy, love. . .because of these I can put my trust in You. Your power surpasses anything man-made. I know that You can take any circumstance and make good come from it. I can count on You to see me through any difficulty, to hold my hand when I am hurting, and to guide my path through all uncertainties. Help me, Lord, to lean on Your strength and ability to save, not my own. "But when I am afraid, I will put my trust in you" (Psalm 56:3 NLT).

Lord, I cry with the psalmist, "Give me understanding and I will obey your instructions; I will put them into practice with all my heart" (Psalm 119:34 NLT). Amen.

Everlasting Kingdom

There Christ rules over all forces, authorities, powers, and rulers.
He rules over all beings in this world and will rule in the future world
as well. God has put all things under the power of Christ, and for
the good of the church he has made him the head of everything.

EPHESIANS 1:21-22 CEV

Our Father in heaven, the governments in this world give all the appearances of strength and dominance. It's easy for us to forget, when we hear of leaders who abuse their power, that You created every throne and every dominion. You set rulers in their positions of authority. Some as a blessing for us, and others as punishment for turning away from You.

When we try to be kings in our own little corners of the world, we often pay the price of making our situations worse. Then You call us back, reminding us to give our lives back to You. Even when Your resolution isn't the one we prefer at that moment, we usually see in hindsight that Your solution was perfect.

The peace of Christ could rule, mediate, or resolve every situation of our lives, if only we would allow it. As Christ rules over all kingdoms and nations, I pray that we remember to let Him rule in our hearts and minds.

Thank You, Father, for Your gracious kingdom!

I pray this in the name of our righteous and loving King, Jesus Christ, whose kingdom is everlasting. Amen.

Through faith WE UNDERSTAND THAT THE Worlds WERE FRAMED by THE Word of God.

HEBREWS 11:3

God's Handiwork

Come, let us sing for joy to the Lord; let us shout aloud to the Rock of our salvation. Let us come before him with thanksgiving and extol him with music and song. For the Lord is the great God, the great King above all gods. In his hand are the depths of the earth, and the mountain peaks belong to him. The sea is his, for he made it, and his hands formed the dry land. Come, let us bow down in worship, let us kneel before the Lord our Maker; for he is our God and we are the people of his pasture, the flock under his care.

PSALM 95:1-7 NIV

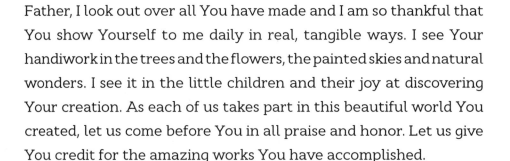

Father, I look out over all You have made and I am so thankful that You show Yourself to me daily in real, tangible ways. I see Your handiwork in the trees and the flowers, the painted skies and natural wonders. I see it in the little children and their joy at discovering Your creation. As each of us takes part in this beautiful world You created, let us come before You in all praise and honor. Let us give You credit for the amazing works You have accomplished.

The joy You've placed in my heart makes me want to sing and shout aloud to all the earth. Thank You for my church where I have the ability to sing and proclaim Your name out loud with fellow believers. You are great, oh Lord. Thank You for all You have done. Amen.

My Prince of *Peace*,

I worship & honor you.

Hands and Feet

*The church, which is his body, the fullness
of him who fills everything in every way.*

Ephesians 1:22–23 niv

Dear Father, it's easy to think of You as distant. Because I can't see You, it seems at times like You're not really here. When I don't have a physical representation of Your love, I feel alone.

But that's not the way it's supposed to be, is it, Lord? You designed the Church to be Your body. You designed churches to give hugs to the lonely, to fix meals for the hungry, to run errands for the invalid.

The Church. . .that's me, isn't it? I'm a part of Your Church. That means I'm a part of Your body. It's my job to be Your hands and feet and heart on this earth.

Father, I've not always done a good job of being Your flesh-and-blood representation. I become absorbed in my own world, my own needs, and I forget to offer myself to others. Please forgive me, and help me love the people You've placed around me in real, flesh-and-blood, up-close-and-personal ways.

Show me practical things I can do, whether it's a hug or a smile or a meal. Perhaps I can make a phone call to let someone know they matter, or wheel their trash can to the curb. The possibilities are endless.

Show me, Lord. Help me. I want to be Your hands and feet in this world. Amen.

Giving Thanks for Jesus

And we know that the Son of God has come, and he has given us understanding so that we can know the true God. And now we live in fellowship with the true God because we live in fellowship with his Son, Jesus Christ. He is the only true God, and he is eternal life.

1 JOHN 5:20 NLT

Dear God, what an amazing gift You gave us in our Lord, Jesus Christ! The prophets foretold His coming. Through them You prepared the world for Your advent. You came in flesh as the Son. You came as Jesus, the child, born in humble surroundings but with such power that angels arrived to slay the darkness. Your star revealed that light had come into the world. Christ lived as He was born, in humility, yet with all of Your power and strength. He healed the sick, walked on water, and performed miracles that only You can do. Each word He spoke had purpose and meaning. His words, Your words, transcend time. We read them in our Bibles and trust in their wisdom. Oh, thank You, God, for Jesus!—God in skin, One like us, speaking to us, living with us, teaching us, and loving us as only You can love. He saved us by Your grace. He washed away our sin and gave us the promise of eternal life. He is with us now and forever. Oh God, thank You so much for Jesus. Thank You for Your wonderful gift! Amen.

In Everything GIVE THANKS.

1 Thessalonians 5:18

Rejoice, Pray, and Give Thanks

Rejoice always, pray continually, give thanks in all circumstances;
for this is God's will for you in Christ Jesus. Do not quench the Spirit.
Do not treat prophecies with contempt but test them all; hold on to
what is good, reject every kind of evil. May God himself, the God of peace,
sanctify you through and through. May your whole spirit, soul and
body be kept blameless at the coming of our Lord Jesus Christ.
The one who calls you is faithful, and he will do it.

1 Thessalonians 5:16-24 niv

Heavenly Father, there are definitely times when I do not feel like giving thanks. Especially when life seems overwhelming. Please forgive me for the stress and anxiety that I allow to consume me. I ask that You carry my burdens and that You would give me the strength and ability to be thankful in every circumstance.

Remind me of Your presence in my life at all times, not just in times of trouble. I know You want to share all of life with me. Yes, You're there for me in hard times, but You want to rejoice with me in good times too. You are a good and faithful God that offers me peace in anything I face. I praise You for Your faithful, unfailing love. Give me the strength and willingness to hold on to all that is good in my life and to reject any evil that comes my way.

Keep my life,

for I am faithful to You.

You are my God.

Psalm 86:2

Delighting in Differences

There are different kinds of spiritual gifts, but they all come from the same Spirit. There are different ways to serve the same Lord, and we can each do different things. Yet the same God works in all of us and helps us in everything we do. The Spirit has given each of us a special way of serving others.

1 Corinthians 12:4-7 cev

Dear Lord, help me to love the diversity among Your people and the diversity among the gifts You have given us. I get self-centered too often and expect that every fellow Christian should be more like me, but that's not right at all! Help me not to compare and contrast my strengths and weaknesses with others. I sometimes judge and criticize.

I sometimes become jealous over what I can't do well and prideful over what I can. Instead, please help me to only compare myself with You. I want to celebrate the fact that You have given us all different gifts and we can use them to serve You and serve others in very different ways. I can't possibly know how You use each different person to further Your kingdom, but I praise You that You do!

Please remove all pride and jealousy from me, and help me focus on wanting to be like You, Jesus, not like anyone else. Help me to discover and develop my own spiritual gifts with the right attitude. I want to use them for Your glory. Amen.

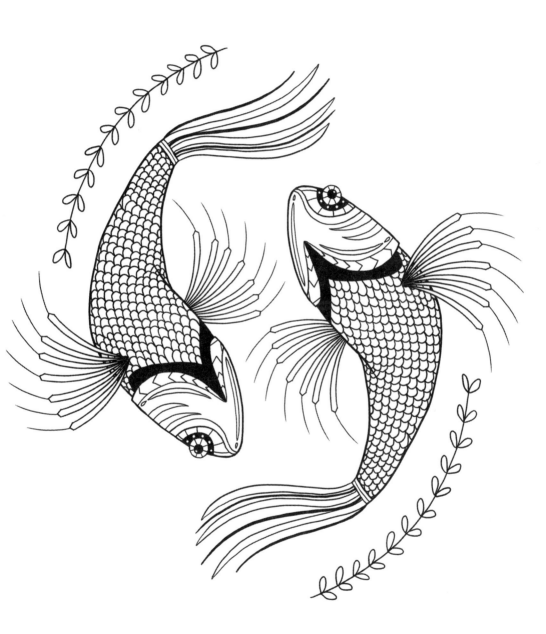

Sweet Anointed Feet

And hath put all things under his feet, and gave him
to be the head over all things to the church.

EPHESIANS 1:22 KJV

Heavenly Father, we often balk at the notion of being considered someone else's lowly footstool. We take offense at people who figuratively wipe their muddy shoes on us, using our backs as a springboard for their own worldly successes.

Please help us to see there is a huge difference between being under the oppressive feet of another person, whose thoughtless actions are for selfish gain, and being under the divine feet of Christ, where we find a calming shelter from the world's negative influences. Give us the unpretentious attitudes of the two women mentioned in the New Testament who washed and anointed Jesus' feet. They were willing to humble themselves in His presence. Both women trusted this man from Galilee—one had faith in His authority to forgive, the other believed in His power over death.

Thank You, Lord, for giving me that hope of Your forgiveness and the belief in eternal life.

I pray, dear Lord, that You will let me be a small footstool for Christ, to live beneath the shadow of His splendid radiance. Oh, that I could weep enough tears from my own repentance to bathe His feet and anoint them with the sweet perfume of my joyful heart!

I pray all things in His name. Amen.

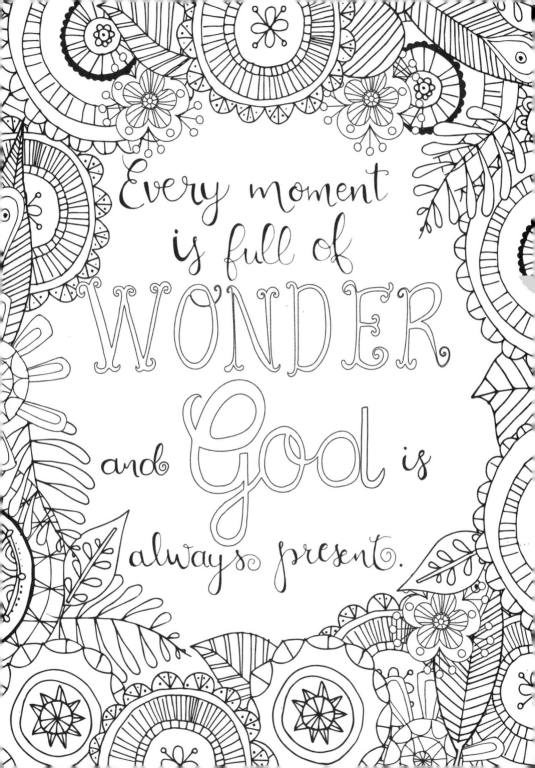

Absolutely True

For we were not making up clever stories when we told you about the powerful coming of our Lord Jesus Christ. We saw his majestic splendor with our own eyes when he received honor and glory from God the Father. The voice from the majestic glory of God said to him, "This is my dearly loved Son, who brings me great joy." We ourselves heard that voice from heaven when we were with him on the holy mountain. Because of that experience, we have even greater confidence in the message proclaimed by the prophets. You must pay close attention to what they wrote, for their words are like a lamp shining in a dark place—until the Day dawns, and Christ the Morning Star shines in your hearts. Above all, you must realize that no prophecy in Scripture ever came from the prophet's own understanding, or from human initiative. No, these prophets were moved by the Holy Spirit, and they spoke from God.

2 Peter 1:16-21 nlt

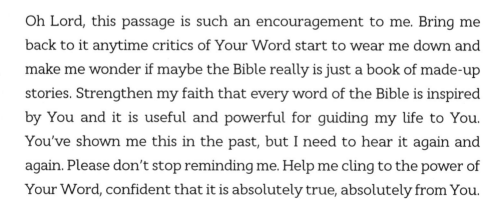

Oh Lord, this passage is such an encouragement to me. Bring me back to it anytime critics of Your Word start to wear me down and make me wonder if maybe the Bible really is just a book of made-up stories. Strengthen my faith that every word of the Bible is inspired by You and it is useful and powerful for guiding my life to You. You've shown me this in the past, but I need to hear it again and again. Please don't stop reminding me. Help me cling to the power of Your Word, confident that it is absolutely true, absolutely from You.

HE IS THE ONE
WHO MADE HIS
LIGHT SHINE
IN OUR HEARTS.

2 CORINTHIANS 4:6

Let Your Creativity Continue With. . .

Daily Wisdom for Women Devotional Coloring Book

Fifty-two encouraging devotional readings complemented by fifty-two unique coloring images on quality stock will comfort and delight through beautiful design and refreshing insights. As women read the weekly devotional, meditate on the scriptures, and unlock their creativity through coloring, they will be drawn to experience an intimate connection to the heavenly Father.

Paperback / 978-1-68322-008-4 / $9.99

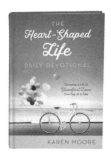

The Heart-Shaped Life Daily Devotional

Readers will be motivated to live a "heart-shaped" life with this daily devotional from Barbour Publishing. With refreshing thoughts, prayers, and scripture selections, *The Heart-Shaped Life Daily Devotional* will help readers discover the best path to the good life. . .which is LOVE.

Hardback / 978-1-68322-009-1 / $14.99